Buy a Used RV for Sale at a Bargain Price

Step-by-step guide shows how to buy a used RV or used motorhome or used campers for sale or even pop up campers for sale well-under current NADA RV market value

By Dagny Wasil

ISBN: 9781980636274

Published by: BookSpecs Publishing, 16 Sunset Ave., Pennsville, NJ 08070

Legal Notice

Your Free Gift

As a way of saying thanks for your purchase, I'm offering a free RV Inspection Checklist to my readers.

This checklist summarizes things that need to be inspected (as discussed in chapter 5 of this eBook) BEFORE you buy any RV.

If you're really interested in buying a used RV then this checklist is yours FREE. It's downloadable in pdf format. Just download it to your mobile device or PC (where you can also print it out).

Having this checklist will make it easy for you to inspect any RV, step-by-step, so you can inspect cosmetic, functional and mechanical components of any RV you're thinking about buying.

You can download this checklist at: www.RvLivingToday.com/checklist.html

www.RvLivingToday.com/checklist.html

Table of Contents

INTRODUCTION

Getting In On the Fun

The RV or "recreational vehicle" concept has been around much longer than many people realize. Covered wagons helped pioneers travel across the North American continent and the idea of living within a traveling vehicle has never really left since that time. They may have been called "caravans" back then, but the idea of mixing travel and home is the same.

The earliest known "motorhome" seems to have been built in Canada around 1910. But the RV market was firmly established in the US by the 1920s, in spite of limited campgrounds and few well-paved roads.

Not long after the auto industry took off, a number of mom and pop operations started springing up, here and there, in order to produce "house trailers" and "coaches." And 1950s postwar prosperity in the US saw the development of large, fully self-contained "motorhomes."

A large and ever-growing number of people are interested in RVs today. Many seniors have discovered new found freedom in the RV lifestyle. Many are "snowbirds" who flee winters up north in order to seek out warmer weather down south. But adults of all ages, including younger moms and dads, are also now incorporating RVs into newer models of living.

Some RVers are "workampers," who work at campgrounds and RV parks in exchange for reduced site fees and thus enjoy a much lower cost of living. Others consider themselves "digital nomads," who take advantage of the power of computing and widespread Internet access in order to travel and earn a living wherever their heart desires at any given time.

Whether you're someone who wants to simply enjoy vacations in an RV, or live in one either full or part-time, this eBook can help you find an RV that perfectly suites your tastes, matches your particular goals, and fits inside your individual budget. Let's get started.

WHY YOU WANT TO BUY A USED RV
How Much Does It Really Cost?

"So, how much does it cost to buy and live in an RV?" This is one of the first questions people ask. And as you might imagine, the answer widely differs, depending upon what kind of RV someone wants and how they intend to use it.

There is probably an RV out there for just about any budget. The biggest challenge to becoming an RVer, however, may not be "knowing the marketplace" but rather "knowing thyself."

There are some very nice used RVs out there selling for as little as $5,000 to $15,000. It's unlikely, however, that most of these will compare to newer motorhomes selling in the $100,000 to $250,000 price range.

If you're new to recreational vehicles then the most important piece of advice I can offer you is, "Don't buy a brand new RV for your first RV." There is a bit of a learning curve when it comes to them and buying new often means vastly overpaying for things you don't really need or may not even want.

New motorhome dealers often set the retail price at 25% higher than the vehicle is worth, right off the bat. In other words, you could negotiate the price downward by 25%, and the dealer would still make money on the sale. Always remember that new RV prices are significantly marked up.

Retail prices on new motorhomes are often listed as much as 25% to 30% more than the RV is worth (even brand new). So this means you'd need to negotiate at least a 25% to 30% discount at the outset of a purchase from the dealer in order to avoid a huge loss if you wanted to sell it within a few years.

So here is the bottom line...

If you'd like to acquire a very nice RV and get a very good deal on it at the same time then there are plenty of available used RVs out there (at bargain rates). We're going to discuss all of this so you're equipped to make the best decisions on these matters moving forward.

New Versus Used

New RVs depreciate in value very quickly. Buying new can be a very costly mistake, especially for someone who buys a particular class or model and then decides they don't really want it anymore and desire to quickly sell it. Such an individual is probably going to lose a lot of money within a short space of time.

For some folks, there may be some advantages to buying a new RV. If a person has accumulated the experience to know exactly what type of model they really want and they plan on keeping it for many years then negotiating a good retail price with an RV dealer might be the right decision. At this point in their lives, they've got the experience (and wisdom) to go through that process without coming out on the short end of the stick.

Ironically, one very good reason for NOT buying new is a desire to avoid RV maintenance issues. Buying a new RV is not like buying a new car. New car buyers pretty much assume (correctly) that acquiring a new car will help them avoid most, if any, vehicle maintenance problems. Not so with RVs.

Even new RVs frequently need to have certain things fixed. While a good number of them may be included in a dealer's warranty package, getting a problem resolved may prove to be a hassle. And if you happen to be away on a trip in a new RV when something breaks then a quick fix is likely going to be impossible.

Here are some general advantages and disadvantages of buying new versus buying used RVs:

 Buying New (Advantages):

-- Receive a limited warranty to cover any manufacturer problems

-- Ability to obtain financing with monthly payments (dealers try hard to make it easy to buy as quickly as possible)

-- Bonus memberships to campgrounds and/or RV travel associations

-- Complete RV walk-through with detailed explanations on how everything works

Buying New (Disadvantages):

-- Limited RV models to choose from at the dealer

-- Quick monetary depreciation from full retail price (as much as 15% as soon as a new RV buyer drives the RV off the dealer's lot)

-- New buyers often owe (in payments, for many months [and sometimes years] after purchasing) more than their RV is currently worth on the used market

-- Pay substantially more than a similar model RV that is slightly used

-- Generally higher monthly payments (that often go on for a much longer period of time)

-- Need to repair any manufacturer problems discovered during early usage after purchasing

Buying Used (Advantages):

-- Huge selection of choices on the used market

-- Acquire any particular make/model RV at a substantially lower price

-- Search and locate for an RV that has all the exact features you really want

-- Possibly acquire expensive upgrades in the RV that its existing owners have already paid for

Buying Used (Disadvantages):

-- Possibility of acquiring mechanical/maintenance problems not covered by any warranty

-- No 100% guarantee of RV history or existing condition

-- Existence of general exterior and interior "wear and tear"

-- Possible need to replace certain expensive items immediately (such as tires or batteries)

-- No seller financing (any financing must be arranged beforehand in order for sale-purchase to be transacted)

In my humble opinion, the reasons to buy used far outweigh the reasons to buy new.   If you have some patience, are willing to do a bit of research and then are also willing to pull up your sleeves in order to thoroughly inspect the condition of any used RVs that really appeal to you, then you're going to be in a very good financial position when it comes time to buy.   Buying used can save you anywhere from thousands to tens of thousands of dollars in the long run.

At best, you'll enjoy your RV at lower cost than if you'd bought it brand new. At worst, you'll discover it wasn't the perfect RV for you after all. But now you'll be in a position where you can probably sell it for at least the amount you paid for it (and maybe even a good bit more).

If you're just starting out on the journey of becoming an RVer, however, then I still DO strongly suggest you visit many new RV dealers. (Just don't get seduced by their sophisticated marketing methods).

So why am I saying you should visit lots of RV dealerships? To learn.

Discover what makes, models and features you really want in an RV. Read about the various classes available, see different floor plans, and step inside both large and tiny bathrooms.

Make it an adventure. Start keeping your own notebook. Take lots of pictures (perhaps even video). And begin thinking through how what you really want should be linked to how you plan on using your RV.

Let's explore much more on this in our next chapter.

RV CLASSES / TYPES
Different Classes and Types of RVs

As you begin searching for a "perfect RV," it becomes evident that RVs are categorized into distinct classes (i.e., classifications) and types. Each kind will probably be immediately recognizable to most people.

It's important to note, however, that one really needs to investigate each kind of RV personally in order to really know the benefits and drawbacks of each sort of dwelling. Technically speaking, Class A, Class B and Class C RVs are also referred to as "motorhomes."

Class A Motorhome: These are the largest motorhomes. They may appear to be elegant commercial buses on the outside. They typically feature beautiful interiors to match. Their amenities may include multiple bedrooms, spacious bathroom(s), "slide out" room(s), roomy kitchen area, full-scale appliances and lots of storage areas.

Class A motorhomes get about 7 to 9 mpg and are generally easier to drive than the larger travel-trailer type RVs (discussed a few paragraphs down). They're the most expensive type of RV to buy new and their monetary value often depreciates very rapidly. There are many good buys out there on some very nice Class A motorhomes if you're willing to search them out.

Since they offer so much room and creature comforts, Class A motorhomes are often the preferred choice of both retirees and those with families who want lots of personal space.

Class B Motorhome: Class B's are the smallest kind of motorhome. They're often called "camping vans" because that is essentially what they are – large vans with living space in the cab area of the vehicle.

Despite the small living space in these RVs, Class B motorhomes are the most popular class nowadays. They're easy to drive (similar to driving a large SUV), can be parked anywhere and get the best gas mileage (15 to 17 mpg) among motorhomes.

These motorhomes are ideal if you plan on traveling a lot but not living in one full-time. Since these motorhomes are the most popular class these days they tend to be very expensive when sold brand new, but they depreciate much more slowly and command hire re-sale prices for used ones.

In other words, their pricing reflects the law of "supply and demand." That being said, there are still some very good buys out there for a Class B motorhome, depending on your budget.

Class B RVs are great for individuals and couples willing to share a small space. And they can easily be used as a "second car" in some families.

Class B+ Motorhome: This is the newest class of motorhome on the market today. It's essentially the end of a van built on a truck chassis. They do not, however, possess the "over the head bunk area" seen on Class C motorhomes (featured in the paragraphs below).

They offer a somewhat larger living space than standard Class B vans, get better gas mileage than Class C motorhomes, generally reflect high quality building standards and are becoming very popular in today's marketplace.

The growing popularity of Class B+ RVs means they're very expensive when bought new and hold their resale values when sold as used. In other words, they depreciate much slower than Class A or Class C motorhomes.

Class C Motorhome: These are among the most common motorhomes seen on the road today. They often look similar to U-Haul moving trucks, with exterior van built on a truck chassis and extension (sleeping bunk) over the cab. In short, this is the ubiquitous cab-camper seen on highways all across North America.

Small families have enjoyed Class C motorhomes for many decades. They're a long-standing part of the camping tradition associated with the RV movement.

Although Class C motorhomes are often more spacious and less expensive than Class B motorhomes they depreciate in value very quickly after a new buyer pays the expensive listing price for a brand new one. One notable problem that has afflicted many Class C motorhomes is leakage around the seams of the cab extension area. They're also less aerodynamic than Class B motorhomes, which means they don't get great gas mileage.

Fast depreciation means there are many Class C motorhomes available at bargain rates. This includes ones with low mileage.

Trailer / Camper RVs: Trailer-campers (or camper-trailers, depending upon your preference of terminology) come in a wide variety of sizes with as many features as one might imagine. As rectangular-shaped boxes on wheels they can range from very cramped to generously spacious, one tiny living space to multiple rooms, and no slide-outs to several slide-out areas.

While very small campers can be pulled by a car, larger ones are in need of a truck. Unless one already has a truck this cost needs to be figured in with the cost of the camper. And one thing you always need to do is properly determine the weight towing capacity of the truck. Be sure it's rated for the weight of the RV you eventually buy.

Trailers are harder to maneuver on the road than a van or bus. They can also be very challenging to handle when backing up. A good deal of experience is usually required before a driver begins feeling comfortable towing a trailer behind them, especially a larger one.

In general, trailer-campers see their value depreciate rapidly over the course of the first few years of their life. Buying used is always the way to go if you want a deal on this type of RV.

Fifth-Wheel RVs: These RVs are large camper-trailers with one additional standout feature – a large overhand on the front end called a "gooseneck." This gooseneck connects the trailer to a large swiveling base hitch located inside the bed of the large pickup truck that is required to tow it.

Fifth-wheel RVs can be huge. Many of them feature a large bedroom inside their gooseneck area, and many have a second bedroom in the rear of the trailer. (When it comes to fifth-wheels, be especially sure to note the truck towing capacity, as mentioned in the above paragraphs on "trailer-camper" RVs.)

Like Class A motorhomes, fifth-wheels can be both luxurious and a bad investment. If you buy used, however, real bargains are possible. It's just that you'd probably want to buy with a long-term view in mind since the unit will likely depreciate significantly the longer you hold onto it.

Truck Camper (a.k.a. Slide-In) RVs: These are very small RVs that fit into the bed, up onto the back of a pickup truck. While some may contain a small sink, cook stove and refrigerator, the main function of this type of RV is to offer the truck's passenger(s) an area to sit down and sleep in.

The biggest challenge with slide-in type campers is they tend to make the vehicle unstable. Many owners either sell or trade in this type of RV because they're very uncomfortable driving with them. As soon as a truck camper gets loaded with gear the added weight can really affect the driving vehicle's center of gravity.

As you can imagine, the owner of a slide-in unit that isn't very happy with the affect such a camper has on the ability to drive safely may be willing to unload it for much less than he or she paid for it. Before buying one you always want to be sure you're aware of how the unity handles on the road.

Pop-Up (a.k.a. Fold-Down) Trailer RVs: Pop ups offer owners a lightweight version of trailer camping. The big difference is their tent-like covers spill out over the sides in order to provide roomy sleeping areas.

Pops ups can be quite roomy, depending upon how large the trailer base structure is. Many are equipped with stoves, small refrigerators and even small shower areas.

One disadvantage of pop-ups is their tent fabric tends to eventually succumb to mildew and rot. And while they are a step up from simple tent camping, pop-ups don't feature hard, insulated walls that clearly create an "inside environment" as opposed to the "outside environment." This makes pop-ups a popular choice for budget-conscious families in search of short-term backyard parties and camping trips.

In general, pop-ups can lose their value quickly in the marketplace. The condition of the tent fabric on such a unit will greatly affect the RV's appearance. If you've got a mind to buy a used one in order to keep it long-term then resale value won't be as much of a concern.

Hybrid RVs: These are worth a mention only in the fact that they exist. Many variations and forms of "hybrid" type camping enclosures can be found nowadays.

While there may be some commercial hybrid RVs in existence a good number of them have been built by DIYers trying to save a few bucks. And while it's certainly possible many DIY units are well-built, it can be very hard for a potential buyer to access such a hybrid RV's condition because it's unique and without comparison. It's difficult to access a "market value" to things where an extremely limited market exists.

Let's now turn to the subject of how to search for the particular RV Class or Type you're really interested in owning. Your primary search tools are going to be some websites you may already be a little familiar with. On to the next chapter.

Which RV Class / Type is Best for You?

This can only be determined by your own tastes and also by answering questions like the following:

-- How many people does it need to accommodate?

-- Do you plan on simply using it for short camping trips, long camping excursions, to live in part-time or as a full-time residence? (In short, how important is the "livability" of the unit?)

-- Do you plan on primarily staying in campgrounds, hopping around national parks or parking at night in quiet, indiscreet venues while traveling hither and yon?

-- Do you want a motorhome or trailer or slide-in? (If trailer, do you already have a vehicle that is capable of towing it ... and if not, can you afford to buy a vehicle that can?)

-- Do you plan on keeping the RV long-term or do you want to re-sell it after a few years? (Consider how much the class or type of RV you choose is likely depreciate in value)

-- What is your budget? (How much money will be required to buy and maintain the RV? More on this in the next chapter.)

-- How much will it take to insure your RV after buying it? (Do NOT be surprised about this. Call your vehicle insurance company to get an estimate BEFORE PURCHASING any RV).

Visit as many RV dealers in your area as Possible

This is the fastest way to become familiar with the different classes and types of RVs available. Walk through them. Ask as many questions as you can.   Take pictures (even video clips). Take notes.

Write down any features that really stand out to you, especially ones you think that you'll absolutely want to have in the RV you eventually purchase.   Treat every visit to an RV dealership as a fact-finding mission. Have fun with it … just be aware of that sophisticated sales techniques will be employed in order to get you to "buy today." If you can resist such sales tactics then visiting dealerships will be one of your best sources for RV education.

Visit as many RV Shows as Possible

When searching out the ideal RV for you make it a general practice to visit as many RV shows as you can. RV shows are often so fun because they're jam-packed with all types of RVs and you also get to see many brand new industry-related products and services. Even if you have to travel to another nearby state to get into a really big RV show (that won't be coming to your local area) then it may be worth the trip.

Many of the people you meet at RV shows are fountains of knowledge you might need to tap in the near future in order to get more information about something. Be sure to collect the business cards offered to you, in addition to taking your camera (and/or video) and RV notebook.

Just remember that the purpose of RV shows is to "sell" new RVs, not just display them. You're not going to get such an extraordinary deal on a brand new RV at a trade show that it will negate the bargain-hunting tactics we're going to talk about in the next chapters.

SEARCHING FOR AN RV DEAL

Researching RVs ... and Determining Their True Market Value

Let's assume that by now you've got an idea of what type of RV class / type you want. You've visited a bunch of RV dealers, have gone to a number of RV trade shows, and have even checked out some used RVs for sale in your local area to get an idea of the general condition (good and bad) that will be encountered when searching for a used RV.

When researching RVs in general you can also avail yourself to RV clubs and rallies that are held all over the country. Such events are great places to help you really determine what kind of RV is right for you.

Now let's assume for now you're really ready to buy. You've even got a list of some actual makes and models you want to search for sale online that are listed as "used."

Time to research them and determine how much they're actually selling for in the marketplace. Please note that your focus will be on how much they are actually selling for and NOT the prices sellers are asking.

Sellers regularly list RVs for sale at unrealistically high asking prices all the time. Unless the buyer happens to be a complete novice or is simply a person who has lots of extra money (and really wants that particular RV and doesn't care about overpaying for it) then the buyer isn't going to get anywhere near their asking price.

Prior to beginning your search you also want to be sure you know the answer to the following question:

Are you going to keep the RV long-term ... or will you want to sell it in a year or two (or three)?

The reason why you need to be sure about this may affect your buying decision in an important way. You see, if you're sure you will want to just enjoy the RV for a short period of time and sell it in the near future, then you're probably going to want to focus your efforts on buying one that will be EASY TO SELL when you're ready to sell it. And that means buying an RV that is in strong demand.

For example, Class B and Class B+ motorhomes are in very strong demand right now and will probably be in strong demand a couple years from now. That seems to be the trend anyhow. So if you buy a used Class B RV in excellent condition then it will probably be far less difficult to sell it in the near future than it would be to sell a used Class C motorhome. This is the law of supply and demand in action; it's that simple.

Yes, it might mean you'll have to pay a bit more for the RV when buying. But it also means the RV will retain its value far more strongly than one that isn't in demand. The bottom line here is that you want to think about the "bottom line" when it will come time to sell the RV you're about to buy.

If you think you're going to sell the RV at some point then you also may want to strongly consider buying one only from a manufacturer that has a good reputation. You can check out online forums to determine the name brands that have the highest recognition for building quality RVs. Stay away from manufacturers that don't have a strong building track record.

Where and How to Search

Most of the research process will take place online. This will especially be true when it comes to determining the true market value for any RV.

It may be possible the actual RV you eventually purchase might not happen to be listed online, which we will talk a little about at the end of this chapter. But most of our discussion here will focus on using Internet websites to locate a great RV that you'll be able to buy at a great price.

The two primary sites are eBay and CraigsList. Both of these will help you determine the true market value of an RV. But eBay is the most important one for reasons we'll discuss below.

One additional point to keep in mind is the fact that location can really affect the market value of an RV. For example, the same RV for sale on the West Coast of the U.S. might sell for more than it would sell for in a place like Florida. If more RVs are more readily available in one area than another then market pricing can really be affected.

eBay

The #1 site for determining market value for an RV is eBay. Why? Because eBay enables you to see the actual selling prices of RVs that have actually sold in auction.

Remember, many asking prices are pie-in-the-sky and unrealistic. The only things that matter in terms of genuine real-world market value are actual selling prices!

What you need to see are the "Completed Listings" for the exact kind of RVs you're interested in buying. To do this, log into your eBay account and go to the "advanced" tab in the top right-hand of the screen. Click on that link and enter words such as "RV" and "motorhome" etc.

Next, scroll down and click on the icon that says, "Completed Listings." Enter in some sort of minimum number in order to weed out small, unrelated RV related items until you see completed RV auctions. The ones in green will be the ones that actually sold. The red ones will be ones that didn't sell because either the seller's reserve price wasn't met or nobody bid on the RV in the first place (possibly because the seller's listing price was far too high to begin with).

Allow eBay's successfully completed auctions listings show you exactly what the RV you want to buy is selling for right now ... in today's market. Don't pay higher.

You can now use this same pricing valuation as a baseline to try and get a better deal. In other words, use your eBay findings of actual, recently completed auction sales to show you what "below market offer" you can make to a seller who has an RV you'd like to try and buy. To get a great deal on an RV you want to BUY IT FOR LESS THAN what similar RVs are currently selling for on eBay.

Regardless of how much you decide to low-ball a seller to try and get the best possible deal, you simply never want to pay more for an RV than what similar ones are selling for on eBay right now. Allow eBay's current listing of completed auctions prices determine the most you're willing to pay.

START any negotiation with any seller using eBay's actual market value for the RV you want to try and buy from them!

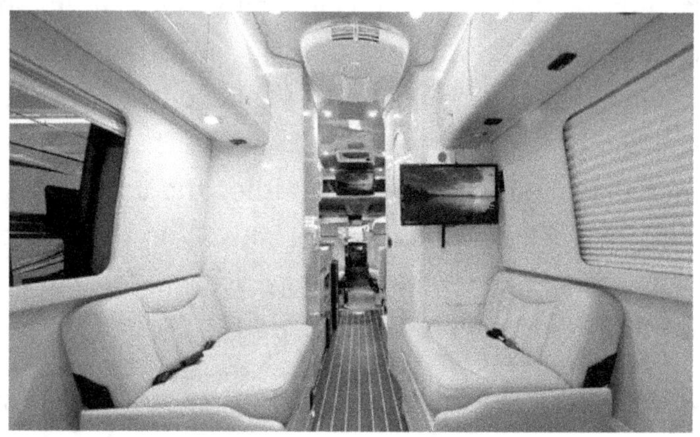

CraigsList

After you've determined what actual market value is for an RV on eBay you can use CraigsList.org and expand your search for it. Remember to search both in your area and outside it to nearby States. And if you're willing to travel even farther to make an offer for any particular RV the better.

Places such as Arizona, New Mexico, Texas and Florida are filled with retirees who are selling their RVs. Many of them will be in great condition and more than a few could be obtained at bargain rates. All it takes is a really motivated seller.

It's also not uncommon for the adult child of someone who has recently passed away to sell their parent's RV as part of settling their estate. Many simply just want to get rid of big items as quickly as possible and don't know (or care to know) the true worth of a used RV. That kind of scenario is a potential buying opportunity.

Also, many senior citizens don't like the idea of selling things on eBay. They will happily list items for sale on CraigsList though because they're very familiar with the idea of classified newspaper ads. CraigsList is currently the 21st century's version of classified advertising. (*Quick word of caution: never pursue any CraigsList ad that doesn't feature a phone number for the seller. Many of these ads are scams.)

One website you might find helpful to use along with CraigsList is www.searchtempest.com … this site can perform an expanded search on CraigsList for any particular RV model. It can show State by State results that includes the RVs' list prices. You'll be able to see how the prices for an RV may be lower from State to State and also spot pricing trends.

If you use a web browser such as Firefox there are a couple of "add-ons" that can make searching Craigslist easier. One is called "Craigslist Helper," and the other is called "CraigsList Fusion." Both can help you scan hundreds of CraigsList ads more quickly. CraigsList Helper even includes ad photos. Just use your favorite search engine to find out more about each add-on, including where they can be downloaded.

Other Websites

There are many websites that list used RVs for sale that aren't listed on either eBay or CraigsList. They'll allow you to search by make, model and price and often list RVs for sale by dealers as well as private owners.

Remember that asking prices are just that – asking prices. You're going to begin your negotiations by offer less than what actual closed sale listings are on eBay. That being said, you may like the list prices on many of the used RVs you see on some of these websites.

Here are a few of the more popular websites to check out used RV listings:

-- http://www.rvtrader.com – Used RV listings website

-- http://rvs.oodle.com/used-rvs/for-sale – Search engine for all local classified ads

-- http://for-sale.yakaz.com – Search engine for all local classified ads

--   http://www.campingworld.com/rvsales   –   Used motorhomes listed at Camping World locations

-- http://www.nadaguides.com/RVs – National Automotive Dealers Association market pricing guides (includes RVs)

Used RVs at Nearby Local Dealers and RV Parks

Research the RV dealerships in your area (you should already know them well based upon your initial RV research to find out what kind of RV is right for you). Now is the time to recheck these dealers to see if they've got any used RVs in the class, make and models you're now interested in buying.

You may also want to drive through any nearby RV parks / campgrounds and check out any RVs that have "for sale" signs posted. Sometimes the owners will be motivated sellers.

Your search efforts will eventually lead to either one or several RVs that match your list. At that point, it's time to begin the process of inspecting to see if it qualifies as a possible purchase.

RV INSPECTION (Prior to Sales Negotiation and Buying)

The Pre-Physical Inspection Phone Call

Before going to physically inspect any RV you'll want to speak with the RVs current owner (or RV dealer selling the used RV) over the phone. This phone call can serve as a "background inspection" for an RV that you may not want to go ahead and take the next step to physically inspect after finding out certain information during this phone call.

In other words, a "pre-physical inspection" phone call will often end up saving you lots of time. A short chat on the phone may result in you being able to remove certain RVs from your current list of qualified choices.

The following are RV background questions to ask the owner / seller prior to setting up a time for any physical inspection of the unit. They are as follows:

-- Do you have a clear title for this RV? (If not then the buying process is going to be very difficult if not impossible … you also want to stay away from an RV with a "salvage title")

-- How much is currently owned on the RV? (If the seller doesn't possess clear title because of existing debt on the RV … and if the seller currently owes more than the RV is worth then forget about buying it if you want a great deal)

-- What is the "general history" of this RV?

-- Is there any rust? (If so then the RV is already in less than "very good" condition)

-- Any broken or cracked windows? (If so then same as above)

-- Has it been used by smokers, i.e., people who smoke? (If so then same as above and it will also probably make it more difficult for you to resell)

-- Is there any water damage or leaks? (If so then same as above)

-- Is the refrigerator / freezer in working order? (If so then same as above)

-- Have any of the RVs original components been removed, or missing? (If so then same as above)

-- Are you familiar with any other problems with this RV?

-- Does generator start easily … and how does it run after it gets going? (How many hours on it?)

-- How many miles-per-gallon do you get with it (if a motorhome)?

-- When was the oil last changed?

-- How new are the tires? (Tires that are more than 5 years old need to be replaced; read more about this below)

-- When was the last time it was taken out on a trip? (An RV that has been sitting unused for at least a year is very likely to possess a good number of maintenance problems / issues. While this may not automatically disqualify it from your list it does mean you may want to consider hiring a qualified RV mechanic to even more thoroughly inspect it. Doing so might save you from unplanned expenses down the road. At the very least, you will want to use any potential problems as bargaining chips to negotiate the seller's price down if you decide to try and buy the RV anyway.)

-- Can you give me the VIN (for a motorhome) so I can run a CarFax.com background check on it?

-- Can you provide some more photos, or even a walk-through video, before I come to see it?

-- What is the current sale price?

-- Where is it located ... and when can we set up a time so I can look at it?

If you're satisfied with the answers to your "pre-physical inspection questions" then the next step is to run the CARFAX or AUTOCHECK Report on it. If that report checks out fine then you're now ready for an all-out physical inspection of the RV.

Prior to Your Arrival

When scheduling a viewing I'll ask the seller to plug the coach into shore-power. And turn on the refrigerator switch and cool down before I arrive. Then, before visiting the seller, I'll search the internet to find similar coaches for sale at lower asking prices. And print those listings to take with me. Having these can help when it comes to negotiating a better price. As a general rule, you never want to view a motorhome while it is raining.

If the RV has "shore power" then ask the seller to plug into it and turn on the refrigerator and any electric appliances / devices well before your arrival time. The fridge should be cold by the time you arrive and everything else should be ready to go.

Take note of the weather. You don't want to inspect an RV when it's raining because it may be harder to see any blemishes on the outside.

Items to bring with you:

-- Eyeglasses (if you need them to read and see clearly)

-- Print outs of the cost of replacement tires for the RV (if the RVs tires are 5 years old and haven't been replaced yet … more on this below)

-- Camera

-- Light work gloves (for hand protection)

-- Blanket to cover the ground (when inspecting underneath the RV)

-- Small Tool Kit (with common tools)

-- Flashlight

-- Small hand-held mirror (to see into any hard-to-access areas)

-- Calculator

-- Notebook, pen

And you also want to print out the following pieces of information in preparation for buying the RV if it passes your inspection ...

-- Print outs of recent eBay auction sale listings of similar RVs that include final bid / purchase prices

-- Print out for a "sales agreement" or "bill of sale" to have ready in case you do make a deal with the seller to buy their RV

Checking Exterior Appearance and Condition

After arriving and meeting the seller ask them for permission to inspect the RV. The first thing you want to do is thoroughly check the outside / exterior of the unit.

Slowly walk around and thoroughly check for the following:

-- Curb appeal (this will be important if you eventually resell the RV in the future)

-- Any sort of body damage whatsoever

-- Cracked or faded paint

-- Rust (visible rust on the exterior often means more rust in hidden areas)

-- Missing / damaged caulking

-- Cracking fiberglass

-- Cracking / flaking paint

-- Dents / scratches

-- Missing parts or pieces

-- Broken glass

-- Missing mirrors

-- Leveling jacks (are they present?)

-- Awning (Is it present and in what condition is it in?)

-- Tires (General condition and pressure of each one. Any cracking?)

-- Tires (Age) … RV tires are marked by a 4-digit number that indicates when the tires were made. The first 2 digits represent the week it was manufactured and the next 2 represent the year. For example, the number "LM, R32 - 13" indicates the tire was made during the 32nd week of 2013)

Checking Interior Appearance and Condition

As you enter into the RV check the following:

-- Doors (Open easily? Close securely? Straight and secure on hinges?)

-- Entranceway steps (Do they work properly?   Are they damaged in any way? Do they extend all the way out?   Do they offer firm, secure footing?)

After entering the interior do the following:

-- Turn on power generator (Easy to start? Any sputtering when running?)

-- Check master control panel (if applicable)

-- Run air-conditioner on "high" to see how generator handles the load

-- Run heater

-- Check ventilation system (if applicable)

-- Turn on water pump (to prepare to run hot and cold water through all of the faucets and showerhead)

-- Turn on propane tank / open gas lines / pilot light

-- Are "slide-outs" present? (If so then test them, move in and out)

You're now inside the interior and can check the following:

-- General cleanliness and appearance of interior living space(s)

-- Odors / smells / signs of mildew, pets or smoking

-- Cleanliness and condition all floors (Any soft spots or damage)

-- Cleanliness and condition any carpeting or floor coverings

-- Cleanliness and condition of ceiling

-- Cleanliness and condition of all appliances

-- Working condition of cabinets, hinges, interior cabinet walls and shelves

-- Cleanliness and condition of any woodwork

-- Cleanliness and condition of walls

-- Signs of any water spots on floors or walls

-- Discoloration and / or water spots in kitchen sink or refrigerator or icemaker

-- Turn on all kitchen sinks

-- Cleanliness and condition of all dining tables and chairs

-- Assembly / disassembly and movement of dinette, chairs and benches (if any)

-- Cleanliness and condition of bathroom

-- Discoloration and / or water spots in bathroom, bathroom counter, faucets, sink, tub or shower

-- Condition and working ability of faucets and tub or shower (turn water on and off)

-- Condition and appearance of toilet

-- Firm floor mounting of toilet (Check for any softness or signs of rotting around toilet floor)

-- Flushing of toilet

-- Condition and size of bedding (or sleeping areas ... are they wide enough? Long enough?)

-- Test couches / beds for usability and comfort (Any broken springs? Rips in fabric?)

-- Check condition of window screens, including movement

-- Windows (Open easily? Close securely? Straight and secure on window tracks?)

-- Check refrigerator temperature

-- Check freezer temperature

-- Light stove burners

-- Check under stove grates (for rust / damage)

-- Inspect and test all interior lighting (switches and lights in all areas)

-- Inspect all fans (switches, blades in all areas)

-- Inspect electrical system further, including any microwave, television and / or stereo sound

If the RV is a motorhome then it's now time to check the driver's cab area. Move into the coach section and check the following:

-- Driver's seat and adjustments (sit and check for comfort and overall condition)

-- Steering wheel (adjustor, working ability)

-- Location and condition of side mirrors (as seen from the inside of the cab)

-- Turn on motor

-- Check door locks

-- Check power windows

-- Blow vehicle's horn

-- Confirm the mileage / odometer reading matches the number advertised

-- Check all dashboard lights, turn signals, gauges and monitors (have working turn signals confirmed by someone also checking outside of the vehicle)

-- Check dashboard air-conditioner

-- Check any remote devices associated with RV operation

Leave motor on and exit the RV (if testing a motorhome). Then check the following:

-- Open hood and check the engine

-- Check engine oil / mechanical fluids

-- Check the condition of belts / blades

-- Look for any fluid / oil leaks underneath

-- Look for any damage to pipes or other parts

-- Look for water dripping from the air-conditioner

If all of these things check out to your satisfaction then the next step is to take a test drive. You never want to purchase any RV unless you've tested it out on the open road in actual driving conditions.

The Test Drive

Depending upon what type of RV you're test-driving, there are a few procedures that can be followed to access how it handles when driving on the road. It's also best for you to act as both passenger and driver during the test drive. There may be things you notice as a passenger - without any distractions – that would be missed if you're the one who is driving.

If you start out as the passenger for the first few miles you can watch the seller and see how they handle the RV. Ask any questions if necessary, and also listen for any sounds that may reveal any potential mechanical problems.

Drive on side roads at first. Determine how the RV handles under normal operation and braking conditions. Then go out onto the highway. Take it up to 65 to 70 MPH (if that is how to typically drive on Interstate roads).   In other words, drive it as you intend to drive it on the highway for long distances.

Does the RV handle well under that speed? How does it feel when passing other vehicles? How does it feel when other vehicles, including large tractor-trailers pass?

If the RV is a motorhome then does it have cruise-control? If so then turn it on and test it out.

Can the RV be easily controlled while driving if you've only got one hand on the wheel? Or do you absolutely need both hands in order to feel like you're in control? If it's hard to handle when cruising down the road then it's not going to be a good purchase.

Imagine driving the RV several long hours at a time. Does the thought of doing that excite … or terrify you? The answer to this question will determine whether or not you should make an offer to purchase the RV.

Other Considerations

The reputation of the RVs builder should always be taken into account. If they don't have an established track record for quality then it may be a riskier purchase than buying an RV from a manufacturer that has a great reputation for quality construction.

Are the RV's tires near (or exceeding) 5 years in age? If so then they need to be replaced because dry rot will eventually set in. RV tires can be expensive and, depending upon the present age of the tires on the unit under consideration, their cost might be a leverage point during any price negotiations with the seller.

Does the RV have a "fresh" appearance and smell within its interior? Can you get a feel as to whether or not the owner really took care of it? Also, remember that mildew is almost impossible to eliminate once it begins. If you can smell mildew then it's a bad sign for as to the general condition of the RV.

When you go into the bathroom does it offer enough room for you to comfortably use it? And can you imagine taking a shower in it at least once or twice a day?

See signs of any "critters." Little rodents (such as mice) often find their way into RVs. If any are present then you're likely to see signs of them near or around the kitchen cabinets (where food is stored).

Go ahead and invest in a title / VIN check. Use a company like CarFax or AutoCheck to get its vehicle report. It's a small investment given the amount of money involved when purchasing an RV.

Are you going to be comfortable with using (or be able to learn how to use) the RV's mechanical systems? Is there anyone you can call for help if you ever have any questions about them?

Are all of the owner manuals / manufacturing books present? If purchased new then a responsible seller will be one who can provide all of the documentation that came with the RV when it was purchased new. (Such documentation may also help you sell the RV in the future).

Is there a maintenance log for the RV? If so then you can confirm its maintenance schedule.

If you lack the expertise to conduct a full mechanical inspection of the RV then either hire someone or bring along a qualified friend. There is no substitute for qualified experience.

If the physical inspection goes well and you're satisfied the RV is in very good condition then you're all set to make an offer to purchase. Let the monetary negotiation begin.

NEGOTIATING A GREAT DEAL ON A USED RV
Prepared to Negotiate

If the RV under consideration passes your inspection requirements then it's time to sit down with the seller and negotiate a great price (for you). If you remain ever polite but very firm in the price you're willing to pay then you stand a very good chance of getting the RV at a bargain rate.

When it comes to being able to make a great deal there is one thing you NEED to do before sitting down to negotiate with any seller: Have either cash or financing IN PLACE at your bank and ready to go.

We're not talking about paying for an RV with a large wad of cash here either. Even if you have the full purchase amount available in cash you're still going to pay for the RV by check. (We'll talk a little more about this at the end of the chapter).

In terms of financing, you want to be somewhat pre-approved, for a certain amount of money, for the type of RV you're going to be buying. Your eBay research should go a long way in helping you achieve this with your bank's managers to a degree. (Again, we'll talk a little more about this at the end of the chapter).

Having cash or financing in place prior to speaking with a seller puts you in a strong buying position. You want the RV seller to know you're a serious buyer who has the means to buy the RV immediately.

Now, let's talk about how you prepare to "talk turkey" with an RV seller.

Since it's impossible to lay out every possible scenario or script out every possible conversation I won't try. There are many books out there on the topic of "making a deal" that, in my opinion, attempt to teach too much.

It's not that I don't appreciate lots of great information, along with a theoretical background regarding its implementation. But how many profound tips mentioned within a large tome opining on the subject of negotiation are you REALLY going to be able to implement in a real-world conversation?

Probably not many. So let's keep things simple and consider general guidelines and talking points.

The Psychology of Baby Steps and Time Investment

One great thing about taking time to inspect the RV, and then taking it for a test drive, is that it creates a psychological reality that can work greatly in your favor. It can also work against you … if you permit it. But that's why we're talking about it here – so you won't let it work against you!

What is this psychological reality?

The principle of taking baby steps until one reaches a point of commitment because of the time invested from them taking those baby steps. It's easy to understand actually.

What happens when you invest time in something in order to reach a particular goal? The more time you invest the more you really want to "win the prize" so to speak.

Time is the most precious investment we can ever make into something. Time spent equates to certain portion of your life that is spent or "invested." The more amount of time someone spends in some kind of goal-achieving activity the less they want to fail to reach that goal.

In our case here, if you're now at the point of trying to make a deal with the seller then the one you're about to negotiate with has already spent (i.e., invested) a bit of time talking to you over the phone and then spent a good deal more time going through your RV inspection and then spent a bit more time taking you for a test-drive.

They've now invested their time into meeting you … getting to know a little bit about you … talking about the RV with you … being with you. They've started down a path to sell the RV to YOU.

They'd REALLY like to complete the sale now simply because of the time they've now invested into your meeting. Closing the sale, for them, means "winning" and "achieving their desired goal."

In your case, the psychology is essentially the same, except with the opposite goal. After taking time out of your life to find, inspect, test drive and now speak to the seller about his or her particular RV, it's very likely going to be difficult for you (meaning emotionally, psychologically) to walk away from the negotiation without buying this particular RV.

This is psychological reality at work!

But you don't want your emotions to RULE over you here … no matter how much you really like that beautiful, gorgeous, wonderful, seemingly-perfect RV sitting just outside the door.

Refuse to allow the psychological influence to control your actions. Just be confident that the same powerful emotional influence that will pressure you to BUY is also being felt by the person sitting across from the table from you who wants to make a deal and SELL the RV so they can achieve their own goal.

This is human nature at work!

Understand it and allow the feelings, in this case, to work in your favor. The best person from which to buy anything (especially a thing in top-notch condition) is from a motivated seller.

If the seller isn't extremely motivated then be prepared to "walk away."

Polite, Friendly, Straightforward Negotiation

If getting the right RV ... and getting it AT A GREAT PRICE is your #1 goal here then being willing to walk away if the seller doesn't want to budge on their selling price won't be hard for you. You always want to be prepared to walk away from an unmotivated seller.   And if this happens, you can always politely give them your contact info so they can reach out to you "if they change their mind" before you buy someone else's RV.

How can you gauge the seller's motivation?

Remember printing out those closed-sale auctions, including the closing bid prices, of similar RVs that recently sold on eBay? Have those print-outs ready and show the seller what their RV is currently worth in the marketplace right now.

Show these to the seller.   Explain what these print-outs show.

Let them know you're willing to purchase the RV "in the range" of these prices. (What you're really going to try and do, of course, is buy the RV for LESS THAN what it's currently worth if you turned around and sold it on eBay next week because this is the FINANCIALLY SAFEST way to buy an RV. And, paying a price that is just below the range of what similar RVs are currently selling for on eBay is THE BEST REAL-WORLD MEASURE as to whether or not you're really getting a good deal).

Start the negotiation with your research of COMPARISON PRICES OF SIMILAR RVs FROM COMPLETED EBAY AUCTIONS. Don't allow your discussion to begin with the seller's likely super-inflated asking price. Your research is proof that what you're willing to pay for the RV is perfectly reasonable.

Used RV prices are much more negotiable than used auto prices. With few exceptions, used RVs are always dropping in value. As we mentioned in a previous chapter, used Class B and Class B+ RVs tend to hold their value much stronger than other RV types in today's market but even their value is going down over time.

Be sure to compliment the owner / seller of the RV. Let them know you understand it's a great RV and that you can see it appears to have been well taken care of but there are a lot of used RVs for sale right now and you are willing to pay $X dollars for it today because, according to your research, it's a very reasonable offer.

At this point, you can show them print-outs of other similar RVs that are for sale right now. Let the seller know you'd really like to buy theirs "today" if he or she agrees to let you buy it for the price you can pay.

Emphasize to the seller that you'd love to buy their RV instead of having to go and look at other ones for sale. Ask them to give you their "best price." Be polite but firm.

Allow the conversation to move slowly. No need to rush it.

Politely state what you're willing to pay for the RV (a price that is well under eBay auction closed sale prices) and then stop talking. Put the ball in the seller's hands. Keep quiet. Allow for silence. Keep the ball in their hands. Let them feel the pressure to drop the price.

Emphasize to the owner that you do have the money, that you'd really love to purchase their RV today and that if they sell you theirs then they won't have to take any more time talking to anyone else about it or wasting time and energy dealing with people who may not even have money to pay.

Also, be sure to point out ANY defect to the seller that you may have uncovered during your RV inspection. If something needs to be fixed or replaced then point out that you're going to have to pay money for it and that is another reason why your offer is a good one.

If they won't budge and come down to the price you're willing to pay then slowly stand up to leave and invite them to contact you if they change their mind. This action will often elicit the effect of moving a reluctant seller to drop the price.

In this way, you're either going to buy the RV at a great price or not. If the seller is unwilling to drop their asking price from what you're willing to pay then politely walk away. There are, in fact, many nice RVs out there. You'll eventually land a great one at a terrific price.

Remember to leave your contact info with the seller and invite them to call you if they change their mind. Remember, if you've got either cash or the ability to get financing to buy then, as a qualified buyer, you've got leverage in this negotiation.

If You Do Make a Deal with the Seller...

In order to complete the RV purchase you'll want to do the following things:

-- Check the title. Make sure its VIN # matches the RVs VIN # and that there are no liens against it.

-- Fill out the "bill of sale" or purchase agreement that you printed out and brought with you to your meeting. This will typically include: RV make, model, VIN #, mileage (if applicable), purchase price, seller's name and address, buyer's name and address, spaces for both seller and buyer to sign. Make a copy of this bill of sale and give it to the seller when you go to the bank (next step).

-- Drive to the seller's bank in order to make payment. Write a check to them to pay for the RV (the seller's bank can verify your check is good and that you have either the cash or financing to back it).

-- Take possession of the RV immediately after paying for it.

-- Arrange for insurance on it before taking it on the road. (See next chapter on this for an insurance tip).

You'll be the proud "new" owner of a lovely used RV.

A QUICK WORD ABOUT RV INSURANCE

Most states require an RV to have insurance on it before it can be driven. You can call your auto insurance company in order to find out how to arrange to get insurance on the RV quickly.

Another option is to use an insurance company such as Progressive, which allows you to quickly sign up online and then print out insurance cards (for proof of insurance coverage). You can find details for them at https://www.progressive.com/rv/

Before driving the RV be sure to check air pressure in all tires. Also, consider joining a RV emergency road service. You can find one such program at http://www.goodsamclub.com/

Now, time to go somewhere ...

WOULD YOU LIKE TO KNOW MORE?

It is true. Florida is one of the most beautiful states in the country. Its sub-tropic climate is conducive to an abundance of flora and fauna, making it a paradise of fruits, flowers and trees.

Buying a used RV, regardless of how much of a wonderful deal you get, still costs both time and money. And it's only a part of the overall picture of RV ownership and enjoyment.

Please visit us at RvLivingToday.com in order to keep up-to-date and stay on the cutting edge of what is going on in the way of "RV Living" today.

You can also go to **www.RvLivingToday.com/kindle** in order to see a complete list of our kindle eBook titles available on Amazon.

And remember to download your free gift …

As a way of saying thanks for your purchase, I'm offering a free RV Inspection Checklist to my readers.

This checklist summarizes things that need to be inspected (as discussed in chapter 5 of this eBook) BEFORE you buy any RV.

If you're really interested in buying a used RV then this checklist is yours FREE. It's downloadable in pdf format. Just download it to your mobile device or PC (where you can also print it out).

Having this checklist will make it easy for you to inspect any RV, step-by-step, so you can inspect cosmetic, functional and mechanical components of any RV you're thinking about buying.

You can download this checklist at: www.RvLivingToday.com/checklist.html

www.RvLivingToday.com/checklist.html

THANK YOU

THANK YOU, dear reader, for purchasing my eBook.

I certainly hope you've found the information here to be both valuable and actionable. I'd also like to invite you to visit RVLivingToday.com and check out any free goodies they may be offering this month.

If you liked this eBook and think others might benefit from it then I need your help. Please take a moment to leave a review for it on Amazon.

Your feedback will help me continue to write the kind of eBooks that help both existing and prospective RV owners get results. If you liked it then please let me know :-)

www.ingramcontent.com/pod-product-compliance
Lightning Source LLC
Chambersburg PA
CBHW060800260726

48660CB00002B/710